Love

A PARALLEL TEXT OF POEMS
FROM THE FILM
Il Postino

Other works by Pablo Neruda in English translation:

Love

Pablo Neruda

POEMS

Translated by
Stephen Tapscott, W. S. Merwin,
Alastair Reid, Nathaniel Tarn,
Ken Krabbenhoft and Donald D. Walsh

THE HARVILL PRESS
LONDON

This selection, compiled by Francesca Gonshaw, first published in the USA by
Miramax Books, an imprint of Hyperion Books, 1995

This edition first published in Great Britain in 1995 by The Harvill Press

14 16 18 20 19 17 15 13

English translation © by W.S. Merwin, 1969
Translated from the Spanish
20 Poemas de Amor y Una Canción Desperada
First published in Santiago de Chile, 1924

Translations © Anthony Kerrigan, W.S. Merwin, Alastair Reid and
Nathaniel Tarn, 1970. Translated in *Selected Poems* by Pablo Neruda
edited by Nathaniel Tarn and published by Jonathan Cape

Copyright © Donald D. Walsh, 1973
Copyright © Stephen Tapscott, 1986
Copyright Ken Krabbenhoft, 1995

The Harvill Press
Random House, 20 Vauxhall Bridge Road, London SW1V 2SA

Random House Australia (Pty) Limited, 20 Alfred Street, Milsons Point
Sydney, New South Wales 2061, Australia

Random House New Zealand Limited, 18 Poland Road, Glenfield
Auckland 10, New Zealand

Random House South Africa (Pty) Limited, Endulini, 5A Jubilee Road
Parktown 2193, South Africa

The Random House Group Limited Reg. No. 954009
www.randomhouse.co.uk/harvill

A CIP catalogue record for this book is available from the British Library

ISBN 1 86046 186 7

Designed and typeset in Spectrum at Libanus Press, Marlborough, Wilts

Printed and bound in Great Britain by Bookmarque Ltd, Croydon, Surrey

Papers used by Random House UK Limited are natural,
recyclable products made from wood grown in sustainable forests. The
manufacturing processes conform to the environmental regulations of the country of origin

Contents

★ ★ ★

BIOGRAPHICAL NOTE

Pablo Neruda was born in 1904 and spent a solitary childhood on the border of the rainforests in Southern Chile. At seventeen, already an accomplished poet, he moved to Santiago to study French literature, and at twenty the publication of his second book, *Twenty Love Poems* & *a Song of Despair* brought him immediate acclaim.

In 1927 Neruda was appointed to the Chilean Consular service and posted to the Orient. Out of the loneliness, alienation and despair of this period came the poems collected in *Residence on Earth*. During his next posting to Spain, he was befriended by a dazzling generation of Spanish poets (Frederico García Lorca, Miguel Hernández, Rafael Alberti) but these years of happiness and productivity were brought to an end by the eruption of the Civil War in 1936. The assassination of García Lorca and other Fascist atrocities propelled Neruda into political activity. Dismissed from his post because of his passionate outspokenness on behalf of the Republicans, from 1939 he served as Chilean consul to Mexico before returning to Santiago in 1943. Already an immensely popular poet and political figure, he was elected Senator in 1945 and joined the Chilean Communist party.

In 1947, Neruda published an open letter accusing the Chilean president of betrayal, Communism was declared illegal and Neruda, pursued by the police, was forced to go into hiding. It was during this time that he wrote *Canto general*, his most celebrated work, which was published on his return to Mexico in 1950.

In the following years, Neruda continued to travel and to write, finally settling in Isla Negra with his third wife Mathilde Urrutia, the muse of his later poems.

In 1971, Neruda returned to Europe as Chilean ambassador to France, representing the government of his old friend Allende. In the same year he was awarded the Nobel Prize for Literature. In 1973, shortly after witnessing the downfall of Allende's regime, Pablo Neruda died of cancer.

Mañana

Desnuda eres tan simple como una de tus manos,
lisa, terrestre, mínima, redonda, transparente,
tienes líneas de luna, caminos de manzana,
desnuda eres delgada como el trigo desnudo.

Desnuda eres azul como la noche en Cuba,
tienes enredaderas y estrellas en el pelo,
desnuda eres enorme y amarilla
como el verano en una iglesia de oro.

Desnuda eres pequeña como una de tus uñas,
curva, sutil, rosada hasta que nace el día
y te metes en el subterráneo del mundo

como en un largo túnel de trajes de trabajos:
tu claridad se apaga, se viste, se deshoja
y otra vez vuelve a ser una mano desnuda.

Morning

Naked, you are simple as one of your hands,
smooth, earthy, small, transparent, round:
you have moon-lines, apple-pathways:
naked, you are slender as a naked grain of wheat.

Naked, you are blue as a night in Cuba;
you have vines and stars in your hair;
naked, you are spacious and yellow
as summer in a golden church.

Naked, you are tiny as one of your nails –
curved, subtle, rosy, till the day is born
and you withdraw to the underground world,

as if down a long tunnel of clothing and of chores:
your clear light dims, gets dressed – drops its leaves –
and becomes a naked hand again.

Me gustas cuando callas

Me gustas cuando callas porque estás como ausente,
y me oyes desde lejos, y mi voz no te toca.
Parece que los ojos se te hubieran volado
y parece que un beso te cerrara la boca.

Como todas las cosas están llenas de mi alma
emerges de las cosas, llena del alma mía.
Mariposa de sueño, te pareces a mi alma,
y te pareces a la palabra melancolía.

Me gustas cuando callas y estás como distante.
Y estás como quejándote, mariposa en arrullo.
Y me oyes desde lejos, y mi voz no te alcanza:
Déjame que me calle con el silencio tuyo.

Déjame que te hable también con tu silencio
claro como una lámpara, simple como un anillo.
Eres como la noche, callada y constelada.
Tu silencio es de estrella, tan lejano y sencillo.

Me gustas cuando callas porque estás como ausente.
Distante y dolorosa como si hubieras muerto.
Una palabra entonces, una sonrisa bastan.
Y estoy alegre, alegre de que no sea cierto.

I like for you to be still

I like for you to be still: it is as though you were absent,
and you hear me from far away and my voice does
    not touch you.
It seems as though your eyes had flown away
and it seems that a kiss had sealed your mouth.

As all things are filled with my soul
you emerge from the things, filled with my soul.
You are like my soul, a butterfly of dream,
and you are like the word Melancholy.

I like for you to be still, and you seem far away.
It sounds as though you were lamenting, a butterfly
    cooing like a dove.
And you hear me from far away, and my voice does
    not reach you:
Let me come to be still in your silence.

And let me talk to you with your silence
that is bright as a lamp, simple as a ring.
You are like the night, with its stillness and constellations.
Your silence is that of a star, as remote and candid.

I like for you to be still: it is as though you were absent,
distant and full of sorrow as though you had died.
One word then, one smile, is enough.
And I am happy, happy that it's not true.

La poesía

Y fue a esa edad ... Llegó la poesía
a buscarme. No sé, no sé de dónde
salió, de invierno o río.
No sé cómo ni cuándo,
no, no eran voces, no eran
palabras, ni silencio,
pero desde una calle me llamaba,
desde las ramas de la noche,
de pronto entre los otros,
entre fuegos violentos
o regresando solo,
allí estaba sin rostro
y me tocaba.

Yo no sabía qué decir, mi boca
no sabía
nombrar,
mis ojos eran ciegos.
y algo golpeaba en mi alma,
fiebre o alas perdidas,
y me fui haciendo solo,
descifrando
aquella quemadura,
y escribí la primera línea vaga,
vaga, sin cuerpo, pura
tontería,
pura sabiduría

Poetry

And it was at that age ... Poetry arrived
in search of me. I don't know, I don't know where
it came from, from winter or a river.
I don't know how or when,
no, they were not voices, they were not
words, nor silence,
but from a street I was summoned,
from the branches of night,
abruptly from the others,
among violent fires
or returning alone,
there I was without a face
and it touched me.

I did not know what to say, my mouth
had no way
with names,
my eyes were blind,
and something started in my soul,
fever or forgotten wings,
and I made my own way,
deciphering
that fire,
and I wrote the first faint line,
faint, without substance, pure
nonsense,
pure wisdom

del que no sabe nada,
y vi de pronto
el cielo
desgranado
y abierto,
planetas,
plantaciones palpitantes,
la sombra perforada,
acribillada
por flechas, fuego y flores,
la noche arrolladora, el universo.

Y yo, mínimo ser,
ebrio del gran vacío
constelado,
a semejanza, a imagen
del misterio,
me sentí parte pura
del abismo,
rodé con las estrellas,
mi corazón se desató en el viento.

of someone who knows nothing,
and suddenly I saw
the heavens
unfastened
and open,
planets,
palpitating plantations,
shadow perforated,
riddled
with arrows, fire and flowers,
the winding night, the universe.

And I, infinitesimal being,
drunk with the great starry
void,
likeness, image of
mystery,
felt myself a pure part
of the abyss,
I wheeled with the stars,
my heart broke loose on the wind.

Walking around

Sucede que me canso de ser hombre.
Sucede que entro en las sastrerías y en los cines
marchito, impenetrable, como un cisne de fieltro
navegando en un agua de origen y ceniza.

El olor de las peluquerías me hace llorar a gritos.
Sólo quiero un descanso de piedras o de lana,
sólo quiero no ver establecimientos ni jardines,
ni mercaderías, ni anteojos, ni ascensores.

Sucede que me canso de mis pies y mis uñas
y mi pelo y mi sombra.
Sucede que me canso de ser hombre.

Sin embargo sería delicioso
asustar a un notario con un lirio cortado
o dar muerte a una monja con un golpe de oreja.
Sería bello
ir por las calles con un cuchillo verde
y dando gritos hasta morir de frio.

No quiero seguir siendo raíz en las tinieblas.
vacilante, extendido, tiritando de sueño,
hacia abajo, en las tripas mojadas de la tierra,
absorbiendo y pensando, comiendo cada día.

Walking around

It happens that I am tired of being a man.
It happens that I go into the tailors' shops and the movies
all shrivelled up, impenetrable, like a felt swan
navigating on a water of origin and ash.

The smell of barber shops makes me sob out loud.
I want nothing but the repose either of stones or of wool,
I want to see no more establishments, no more gardens,
nor merchandise, nor glasses, nor elevators.

It happens that I am tired of my feet and my nails
and my hair and my shadow.
It happens that I am tired of being a man.

Just the same it would be delicious
to scare a notary with a cut lily
or knock a nun stone dead with one blow of an ear.
It would be beautiful
to go through the streets with a green knife
shouting until I died of cold.

I do not want to go on being a root in the dark,
hesitating, stretched out, shivering with dreams,
downwards, in the wet tripe of the earth,
soaking it up and thinking, eating every day.

No quiero para mí tantas desgracias.
No quiero continuar de raíz y de tumba,
de subterráneo solo, de bodega con muertos,
aterido, muriéndome de pena.

Por eso el día lunes arde como el petróleo
cuando me ve llegar con mi cara de cárcel,
y aúlla en su transcurso como una rueda herida,
y da pasos de sangre caliente hacia la noche.

Y me empuja a ciertos rincones, a ciertas casas húmedas,
a hospitales donde los huesos salen por la ventana,
a ciertas zapaterías con olor a vinagre,
a calles espantosas como grietas.

Hay pájaros de color de azufre y horribles intestinos
colgando de las puertas de las casas que odio,
hay dentaduras olvidadas en una cafetera,
hay espejos
que debieran haber llorado de vergüenza y espanto,
hay paraguas en todas partes, y venenos, y ombligos.

Yo paseo con calma, con ojos, con zapatos,
con furia, con olvido,
paso, cruzo oficinas y tiendas de ortopedia,
y patios donde hay ropas colgadas de un alambre:
calzoncillos, toallas y camisas que lloran
lentas lágrimas sucias.

I do not want to be the inheritor of so many misfortunes.
I do not want to continue as a root and as a tomb,
as a solitary tunnel, as a cellar full of corpses,
stiff with cold, dying with pain.

For this reason Monday burns like oil
at the sight of me arriving with my jail-face,
and it howls in passing like a wounded wheel,
and its footsteps towards nightfall are filled with hot blood.

And it shoves me along to certain corners, to certain damp houses,
to hospitals where the bones come out of the windows,
to certain cobblers' shops smelling of vinegar,
to streets horrendous as crevices.

There are birds the colour of sulphur, and horrible intestines
hanging from the doors of the houses which I hate,
there are forgotten sets of teeth in a coffee-pot,
there are mirrors
which should have wept with shame and horror,
there are umbrellas all over the place, and poisons, and navels.

I stride along with calm, with eyes, with shoes,
with fury, with forgetfulness,
I pass, I cross offices and stores full of orthopedic appliances,
and courtyards hung with clothes on wires,
underpants, towels and shirts which weep
slow dirty tears.

Inclinado en las tardes . . .

Inclinado en las tardes tiro mis tristes redes
a tus ojos oceánicos.

Allí se estira y arde en la más alta hoguera
mi soledad que da vueltas los brazos como un náufrago.

Hago rojas señales sobre tus ojos ausentes
que olean como el mar a la orilla de un faro.

Sólo guardas tinieblas, hembra distante y mía,
de tu mirada emerge a veces la costa del espanto.

Inclinado en las tardes echo mis tristes redes
a ese mar que sacude tus ojos oceánicos.

Los pájaros nocturnos picotean las primeras estrellas
que centellean como mi alma cuando te amo.

Galopa la noche en su yegua sombría
desparramando espigas azules sobre el campo.

Leaning into the afternoons . . .

Leaning into the afternoons I cast my sad nets
towards your oceanic eyes.

There in the highest blaze my solitude lengthens and flames,
its arms turning like a drowning man's.

I send out red signals across your absent eyes
that wave like the sea or the beach by a lighthouse.

You keep only darkness, my distant female,
from your regard sometimes the coast of dread emerges.

Leaning into the afternoons I fling my sad nets
to that sea that is thrashed by your oceanic eyes.

The birds of night peck at the first stars
that flash like my soul when I love you.

The night gallops on its shadowy mare
shedding blue tassels over the land.

Angela Adonica

Hoy me he tendido junto a una joven pura
como a la orilla de un océano blanco,
como en el centro de una ardiente estrella
   de lento espacio.

De su mirada largamente verde
la luz caía como una agua seca,
en transparentes y profundos círculos
   de fresca fuerza

Su pecho como un fuego de dos llamas
ardía en dos regiones levantado,
y en doble río llegaba a sus pies
   grandes y claros.

Un clima de oro maduraba apenas
las diurnas longitudes de su cuerpo
llenándolo de frutas extendidas
   y oculto fuego.

Adonic Angela

Today I stretched out next to a pure young woman
as if at the shore of a white ocean,
as if at the centre of a burning star
   of slow space.

From her lengthily green gaze
the light fell like dry water,
in transparent and deep circles
   of fresh force.

Her bosom like a two-flamed fire
burned raised in two regions,
and in a double river reached
   her large, clear feet.

A climate of gold scarcely ripened
the diurnal lengths of her body
filling it with extended fruits
   and hidden fire.

Fábula de la sirena
y los borrachos

Todos estos señores estaban dentro
cuando ella entró completamente desnuda
ellos habían bebido y comenzaron a escupirla
ella no entendía nada recién salía del río
era una sirena que se había extraviado
los insultos corrían sobre su carne lisa
la inmundicia cubrió sus pechos de oro
ella no sabía llorar por eso no lloraba
no sabía vestirse por eso no se vestía
la tatuaron con cigarrillos y con corchos quemados
y reían hasta caer al suelo de la taberna
ella no hablaba porque no sabía hablar
sus ojos eran color de amor distante
sus brazos construídos de topacios gemelos
sus labios se cortaron en la luz del coral
y de pronto salió por esa puerta
apenas entró al rio quedó limpia
relució como una piedra blanca en la lluvia
y sin mirar atrás nadó de nuevo
nadó hacia nunca más hacia morir.

Fable of the mermaid
and the drunks

All these fellows were there inside
when she entered, utterly naked.
They had been drinking, and began to spit at her.
Recently come from the river, she understood nothing.
She was a mermaid who had lost her way.
The taunts flowed over her glistening flesh.
Obscenities drenched her golden breasts.
A stranger to tears, she did not weep.
A stranger to clothes, she did not dress.
They pocked her with cigarette ends and with burnt corks,
and rolled on the tavern floor in raucous laughter.
She did not speak, since speech was unknown to her.
Her eyes were the colour of faraway love,
her arms were matching topazes.
Her lips moved soundlessly in coral light,
and ultimately, she left by that door.
Hardly had she entered the river than she was cleansed,
gleaming once more like a white stone in the rain;
and without a backward look, she swam once more,
swam towards nothingness, swam to her dying.

Oda a la bella desnuda

Con casto corazón, con ojos
puros,
te celebro, belleza,
reteniendo la sangre
para que surja y siga
la línea, tu contorno,
para
que te acuestes en mi oda
como en tierra de bosques o en espuma:
en aroma terrestre
o en música marina.

Bella desnuda,
igual
tus pies arqueados
por un antiguo golpe
del viento o del sonido
que tus orejas,
caracolas mínimas
del espléndido mar americano.
Iguales son tus pechos
de paralela plenitud, colmados
por la luz de la vida,
iguales son
volando
tus párpados de trigo
que descubren
o cierran
dos países profundos en tus ojos.

Ode to a beautiful nude

With a chaste heart,
with pure eyes,
I celebrate your beauty
holding the leash of blood
so that it might leap out
and trace your outline
where
you lie down in my ode
as in a land of forests, or in surf:
in aromatic loam
or in sea-music.

Beautiful nude:
equally beautiful
your feet
arched by primeval tap
of wind or sound;
your ears
small shells
of the splendid American sea;
your breasts
of level plenitude full-
filled by living light;
your flying
eyelids of wheat
revealing
or enclosing
the two deep countries of your eyes.

La línea que tu espalda
ha dividido
en pálidas regiones
se pierde y surge
en dos tersas mitades
de manzana
y sigue separando
tu hermosura
en dos columnas
de oro quemado, de alabastro fino,
a perderse en tus pies como en dos uvas,
desde donde otra vez arde y se eleva
el árbol doble de tu simetría,
fuego florido, candelabro abierto,
turgente fruta erguida
sobre el pacto del mar y de la tierra.

Tu cuerpo, en qué materia,
ágata, cuarzo, trigo,
se plasmó, fué subiendo
como el pan se levanta
de la temperatura,
y señaló colinas
plateadas,
valles de un solo pétalo, dulzuras
de profundo terciopelo,
hasta quedar cuajada
la fina y firme forma femenina?

The line your shoulders
have divided
into pale regions
loses itself and blends
into the compact halves
of an apple,
continues separating
your beauty down
into two columns
of burnished gold, fine alabaster,
to sink into the two grapes of your feet,
where your twin symmetrical tree
burns again and rises:
flowering fire, open chandelier,
a swelling fruit
over the pact of sea and earth.

From what materials —
agate, quartz, wheat —
did your body come together,
swelling like baking bread
to signal silvered
hills,
the cleavage of one petal,
sweet fruits of a deep velvet,
until alone remained,
astonished,
the fine and firm feminine form?

No sólo es luz que cae
sobre el mundo
la que alarga en tu cuerpo
su nieve sofocada,
sino que se desprende
de ti la claridad como si fueras
encendida por dentro.

Debajo de tu piel vive la luna.

It is not only light that falls
over the world,
spreading inside your body
its suffocated snow,
so much as clarity
taking its leave of you
as if you were
on fire within.

The moon lives in the lining of your skin.

Puedo escribir los versos . . .

Puedo escribir los versos más tristes esta noche.

Escribir, por ejemplo: 'La noche está estrellada,
y tiritan, azules, los astros, a lo lejos'.

El viento de la noche gira en el cielo y canta.

Puedo escribir los versos más tristes esta noche.
Yo la quise, y a veces ella también me quiso.

En las noches como ésta la tuve entre mis brazos.
La besé tantas veces bajo el cielo infinito.

Ella me quiso, a veces yo también la quería.
Cómo no haber amado sus grandes ojos fijos.

Puedo escribir los versos más tristes esta noche.
Pensar que no la tengo. Sentir que la he perdido.

Oír la noche inmensa, más inmensa sin ella.
Y el verso cae al alma como al pasto el rocío.

Qué importa que mi amor no pudiera guardarla.
La noche está estrellada y ella no está conmigo.

Eso es todo. A lo lejos alguien canta. A lo lejos.
Mi alma no se contenta con haberla perdido.

Tonight I can write . . .

Tonight I can write the saddest lines.

Write, for example, 'The night is shattered
and the blue stars shiver in the distance'.

The night wind revolves in the sky and sings.

Tonight I can write the saddest lines.
I loved her, and sometimes she loved me too.

Through nights like this one I held her in my arms.
I kissed her again and again under the endless sky.

She loved me, sometimes I loved her too.
How could one not have loved her great still eyes.

Tonight I can write the saddest lines.
To think that I do not have her. To feel that I have lost her.

To hear the immense night, still more immense without her.
And the verse falls to the soul like dew to the pasture.

What does it matter that my love could not keep her.
The night is shattered and she is not with me.

This is all. In the distance someone is singing. In the distance.
My soul is not satisfied that it has lost her.

Como para acercarla mi mirada la busca.
Mi corazón la busca, y ella no está conmigo.

La misma noche que hace blanquear los mismos árboles.
Nosotros, los de entonces, ya no somos los mismos.

Ya no la quiero, es cierto, pero cuánto la quise.
Mi voz buscaba el viento para tocar su oído.

De otro. Será de otro. Como antes de mis besos.
Su voz, su cuerpo claro. Sus ojos infinitos.

Ya no la quiero, es cierto, pero tal vez la quiero.
Es tan corto el amor, y es tan largo el olvido.

Porque en noches como ésta la tuve entre mis brazos,
mi alma no se contenta con haberla perdido.

Aunque ésto sea el último dolor que ella me causa,
y éstos sean los últimos versos que yo le escribo.

My sight searches for her as though to go to her.
My heart looks for her, and she is not with me.

The same night whitening the same trees.
We, of that time, are no longer the same.

I no longer love her, that's certain, but how I loved her.
My voice tried to find the wind to touch her hearing.

Another's. She will be another's. Like my kisses before.
Her voice. Her bright body. Her infinite eyes.

I no longer love her, that's certain, but maybe I love her.
Love is so short, forgetting is so long.

Because through nights like this one I held her in my arms
my soul is not satisfied that it has lost her.

Though this be the last pain that she makes me suffer
and these the last verses that I write for her.

Oda al mar

Aquí en la isla
el mar
y cuánto mar
se sale de sí mismo
a cada rato,
dice que sí, que no,
que no, que no, que no.
dice que sí, en azul,
en espuma, en galope,
dice que no, que no.
No puede estarse quieto,
me llamo mar, repite
pegando en una piedra
sin lograr convencerla,
entonces
con siete lenguas verdes
de siete perros verdes,
de siete tigres verdes,
de siete mares verdes,
la recorre, la besa,
la humedece
y se golpea el pecho
repitiendo su nombre.
Oh mar, así te llamas,
oh camarada océano,
no pierdas tiempo y agua,
no te sacudas tanto,

Ode to the sea

Here, surrounding the island,
there's sea,
but what sea:
it's always
overflowing,
says yes then no,
then no again, and no,
says yes in blue,
in sea spray, raging,
says no and no again.
It can't be still:
it stammers "My name is Sea",
it slaps the rocks
and when they aren't convinced
strokes them and soaks them
and smothers them with kisses
with seven green tongues
of seven green dogs
or seven green tigers
or seven green seas,
beating its chest,
stammering its name.
O sea, this is your name,
O comrade ocean:
don't waste time or water
getting so upset:

ayúdanos,
somos los pequeñitos
pescadores,
los hombres de la orilla,
tenemos frío y hambre,
eres nuestro enemigo,
no golpees tan fuerte,
no grites de ese modo,
abre tu caja verde
y déjanos a todos
en las manos
tu regalo de plata:
el pez de cada día.

Aquí en cada casa
lo queremos
y aunque sea de plata
de cristal o de luna,
nació para las pobres
cocinas de la tierra.
No lo guardes,
avaro,
corriendo frío como
relámpago mojado
debajo de tus olas.
Ven, ahora,
ábrete

help us instead.
We're meager
fishermen,
men from the shore.
We're hungry and cold
and you're our foe.
Don't beat so hard,
don't shout so loud:
open your green coffers,
place
gifts of silver
in our hands;
give us this day our daily fish.

It's what
we all want.
Though made of silver,
glass and moonlight,
it was meant for
the poorest kitchens.
Don't hoard it
greedily
speeding cold
like wet lightning
below your waves.
Come to us now,
open up,

y déjalo
cerca de nuestras manos,
ayúdanos, océano,
padre verde y profundo,
a terminar un día
la pobreza terrestre.
Déjanos
cosechar la infinita
plantación de tus vidas,
tus trigos y tus uvas,
tus bueyes, tus metales,
el esplendor mojado
y el fruto sumergido

Padre mar, ya sabemos
cómo te llamas, todas
las gaviotas reparten
tu nombre en las arenas:
ahora, pórtate bien,
no sacudas tus crines,
no amenaces a nadie,
no rompas contra el cielo
tu bella dentadura,
déjate por un rato
de gloriosas historias,
dando a cada hombre,
a cada

leave it
within reach.
Help us, ocean,
father deep and green,
help us put at an end
to the world's poverty.
Let us
harvest boundless
crops of your lives,
your wheat and grapes,
oxen and ores,
your wet splendour
and submerged fruits.

We know your name,
father sea: seagulls
shriek it over the sands.
So shape up:
don't toss your mane,
don't give us trouble,
don't break your lovely teeth
trying to topple the sky.
Set the grand stories
aside for now,
give us our daily fish,
big or little as you wish,
one for every man,
woman

mujer y a cada niño
un pez grande o pequeño
cada día.
Sal por todas las calles
del mundo
a repartir pescado
y entonces
grita,
grita
para que te oigan todos
los pobres que trabajan
y digan,
asomando a la boca
de la mina:
'Ahí viene el viejo mar
repartiendo pescado'.
Y volverán abajo,
a las tinieblas,
sonriendo, y por las calles
y los bosques
sonreirán los hombres
y la tierra
con sonrisa marina.

Pero
si no lo quieres,
si no te da la gana,

and child.
Prowl the streets
of this wide world
doling out your fish,
now
shouting
shouting
for all to hear,
all the working poor
gathered at the mouth
of the mine
saying:
' Here's old man sea
doling out his fish'.
Then they'll return
smiling
to the darkness: streets
and forests
will be full of smiling people.
The earth
will wear a sea-blue smile.

But
if you're against it,
if it's not to your taste,

espérate,
espéranos,
lo vamos a pensar,
vamos en primer término
a arreglar los asuntos
humanos,
los más grandes primero,
todos los otros después,
y entonces
entraremos en ti,
cortaremos las olas
con cuchillo de fuego,
en un caballo eléctrico
saltaremos la espuma,
cantando
nos hundiremos
hasta tocar el fondo
de tus entrañas,
un hilo atómico
guardará tu cintura,
plantaremos
en tu jardín profundo
plantas
de semento y acero,
te amarraremos
pies y manos,
los hombres por tu piel

wait,
wait for us.
We'll think it over,
we'll put the affairs
of mankind
in order,
big things first
then all the rest.
And
we'll wade in
slicing your waves
with knives of fire.
We'll mount your crests
on electric steeds.
We'll plunge
singing
to the center
of your being.
Atomic threads
will wrap your waist.
We'll dig
plants of steel and cement
in your deep garden.
We'll tie you
hand and foot.
People will spit casually,

pasearán escupiendo,
sacándote racimos
construyéndote arneses,
montándote y domándote,
dominándote el alma.
Pero, eso será cuando
los hombres
hayamos arreglado
nuestro problema,
el grande,
el gran problema.
Todo lo arreglaremos
poco a poco:
te obligaremos, mar,
te obligaremos, tierra,
a hacer milagros,
porque en nosotros mismos,
en la lucha.
está el pez, está el pan,
está el milagro

gliding on your skin.
They'll pull flowers from your side.
They'll fashion a harness,
mount and break you
and take over your soul,
But this will only happen if
we
solve
our problem,
our
greatest problem.
We'll take it
little by little:
we will make you, sea
and earth, we will make you
perform miracles,
because inside us,
inside our struggle,
is our daily bread, our fish
and our miracle.